BABY
SIGN
LANGUAGE

Communicate with Your Baby
Using Simple Hand Signs

by Sarah Christensen Fu

Featuring Miles Fu, Sam Fu, and Ben Fu

Studio Photography by Amber Marlow

THUNDER BAY
P·R·E·S·S

Thunder Bay Press
An imprint of the Baker & Taylor Publishing Group
10350 Barnes Canyon Road, San Diego, CA 92121
www.thunderbaybooks.com

Copyright © 2013 Thunder Bay Press

Developed by The Book Shop, Ltd.

Designed by Tim Palin Creative

Edited by Catherine Nichols

Video photography of Sarah Christensen Fu by Bryan Chang and Karim Tabbaa of Meerkat Media Collective

Video photography of children by Sarah Christensen Fu

Video Editing/Production: Sarah Christensen Fu

Book Photography Credits

Thinkstock: front cover, title page, 29, 31 (top right), 79, 80, 88-89, 99, 100, 109

Sarah Christensen Fu: 4-5, 8, 13-15, 17, 19, 22-26, 34-35, 44, 51, 55, 57, 68-69, 90-91, 108, 117 (top right), 118, 128

Amber Marlow: 28, 31 (bottom left), 32, 36-39, 41-43, 45, 47-49, 52-53, 58, 61-67, 71-78, 81-87, 92-97, 101-107, 110-116, 117 (bottom right), 120-125

Haley Fulop: 70

All notations of errors or omissions should be addressed to Thunder Bay Press, Editorial Department, at the above address. All other correspondence (author inquiries, permissions) concerning the content of this book should be addressed to The Book Shop, Ltd., New York, New York 10010. www.thebookshopltd.com

ISBN-13: 978-1-60710-705-7

ISBN-10: 1-60710-705-8

Printed in China

1 2 3 4 5 17 16 15 14 13

Contents

Introduction

A few months after my twin boys were born, I started reading about baby sign language and decided that I would teach my babies how to sign. My older son, who was three and a half years old when the twins came along, had used a few signs to communicate as an infant. The signs *more* and *eat* had been very helpful with our first child, and I wanted to tap back into the effectiveness of baby sign language and use it even more with a family that was growing exponentially.

Inspired by a vision of a household calmed by easy communication, I researched the signs, printed and hung pictures around the house, and started signing to my five-month-olds. I tried to remember to sign to them each time I gave them a bottle or nursed, opening and closing my fist to make the sign for *milk*. When a certain aroma filled the air, I signed *change* to them before I picked them up, and then again when they lay squirming on the changing table. Of course there were many times that they were too sleepy, in the midst of a tantrum, or otherwise distracted from signing, but we were able to maintain some consistency. I also taught my husband and babysitters how to make all the signs, and worked with my older son on making the signs as well.

The number one thing I learned during these months was patience. Week after week, I signed and signed, and once in a while one of the infants would show a flicker of recognition or flail their hands back at me in some uncoordinated flurry. Even though I know that every child develops differently, I began to grow concerned that my children would not pick up on the sign language.

Then at around nine months, we turned a corner both with fine motor skills and mental comprehension. The twins started clapping in response to my claps, waving in response to my waves, and then, finally, signing *more*, *milk*, and *eat* in response to my signs. Right around their first birthday, we turned another corner and they finally seemed to understand that each word had a sign that corresponded. They began to sign requests for their favorite foods, toys, and activities. We were able to increase their vocabulary and turn signing into a fun game at mealtimes and during playtime.

The vision of an easy household with twin toddlers and a four-year-old is, of course, just a fantasy, but the fact that we all share a signed vocabulary really helps to keep the chaos to a minimum. Thankfully, the twins' ability to communicate with me eased their transition into toddlerhood, and I'm confident that as we approach the "Terrible Twos" they will feel less frustration because they can tell me what they want and need.

Baby sign language was definitely right for my kids, and I highly recommend it to parents, teachers, or caregivers who want to communicate better with infants and toddlers. In this book, I'll share our methods, progress, and stories of our family's personal experience. Readers will also find stories from other families who use baby sign language, along with tips, games, and songs to make signing fun. The flashcards and DVD also included in this kit will help to reinforce and demonstrate the signs. Good luck, and remember—be patient and have fun!

Sarah Christensen Fu

1

What Is Baby Sign Language?

From the moment your baby is born, he or she begins to communicate. First wails turn into early smiles and giggles; grunts and babbles morph into syllables and recognizable words. Unfortunately, the majority of early communication from infants is lost in translation. Imagine, though, that there was a way your baby could tell you when he wanted a bottle or more of his favorite food.

Imagine a preverbal child being able to identify what hurts at the doctor's office or communicate that she wants to sleep even though it is not her usual nap time.

Baby sign language allows for this type of communication! As early as six to nine months of age—well before the age most humans can communicate verbally—babies begin to develop the gross motor skills and language comprehension to imitate

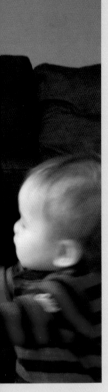

and memorize hand gestures that symbolize things, people, or events in the world around them.

It's easy to teach, and your baby is hard-wired to learn. Most families who attempt sign language are successful and find the experience both fun and valuable.

This book and flashcard set is designed to educate you about baby sign language and help your family get off to a fun and fast start. You'll find facts about the background and widely accepted practices of baby sign language, along with suggestions and tips from real parents who have successfully taught their children. The flashcards can serve to help both you and your baby practice and remember the signs most useful to your family.

Baby sign language gives parents and caregivers the flexibility to adapt or create their own signs and gestures. Most of the signs referenced in this book come directly from American Sign Language (ASL). Using ASL gestures is a common practice among proponents of baby sign language and can be an excellent head start for your child to become fluent in another language.

Origins of Baby Sign Language

1986

More than 100 years later, Dr. Joseph Garcia, an ASL interpreter, noticed that babies as young as six months old were communicating with their deaf parents using ASL. The following year, he began researching using ASL to teach the children of hearing parents.

1755

Abbe Charles Michel de L'Epee of Paris founded the first free school for deaf people, teaching a combination of hand signs and fingerspelling.

1817

Thomas Hopkins Gallaudet, a minister, founded the nation's first school for deaf people in Hartford, Connecticut. By 1863, there were twenty-two schools for the deaf that taught signing and these were the birthplace of American Sign Language.

1998

Kimberlee Whaley conducted the first official baby sign language program, where teachers worked with infants as young as nine months old to communicate using select signs from ASL.

Present Day

Baby sign language is prevalent. There are websites and smartphone apps that demonstrate how to sign to your baby. Many books like this one have been written to help parents get started, and research continues to prove the benefits of teaching babies to sign.

1987

Professor Linda Acredolo noticed her own baby signing and, along with Professor Susan Goodwyn, she began the first long-term study of baby sign language. Twenty years later, their research showed that teaching children baby sign language has significant benefits throughout their development.

Benefits of Baby Sign Language for Families

Baby sign language keeps increasing in popularity because it allows parents and babies to communicate before babies have the developmental ability to speak. Babies can control their gestures at just a few months of age, while it can take eighteen to twenty-four months for infants to master a basic spoken vocabulary.

One of the most important benefits is the bonding time parents get to spend with their infants during the process. Parents and babies love the special attention and the excitement that signing adds to playtime. The shared experience provides context and depth to early communication with a baby and helps parents get to know their child more intimately as new aspects of the baby's personality emerge through signing.

Signing with a child can help prevent and dispel frustration on both ends of the relationship. It's not always easy to guess what will sooth a preverbal child, and signing provides a clear, age-appropriate channel of communication for babies and caregivers. Both the child and the caregiver feel a sense of relief when the baby's needs are met. As infants mature into toddlers, the ability to sign can help them express their more complicated emotions.

Over the last decade, studies have shown there are a great deal of benefits later in life to babies who learned to communicate with signs, including higher IQ and standardized test scores. For more information about these benefits, take a look at studies by doctors Linda P. Acredolo and Susan W. Goodwyn. Information about how to find these studies is in the Resources section in the back of this book.

Additionally, children who learn ASL gain the benefits of being multilingual. Multilingual children can excel in traditional educational environments, and speaking more than one language teaches children that there are multiple approaches to any situation. A study by Laura Berg, listed in the Resources section in the back of this book, shows that preschoolers who learn the signs associated with words are better able to remember words by associating muscle-memory movements with vocabulary.

Like any spoken language, gaining fluency in ASL is a skill that children can continue to perfect through their lifetime, and a skill that will help them communicate better as adolescents and adults.

Combining Signing with Spoken Language

One of the myths surrounding baby sign language is that babies who learn to sign are slower to speak than non-signing babies. Most families who practice baby sign language, however, have found the opposite to be true. One way to help your baby's language development progress alongside the ability to sign is to say each word out loud as you make the sign.

"change"

"milk"

Get Talking!

As your child's signing advances, use their signs as an opportunity to engage them in conversation.

For example, if your baby signs *dog* while out on a walk, you can respond by speaking aloud. "I see the dog, too (sign *dog* back to her as reinforcement). What else do you see on our walk today? Do you see the bicycle? Do you see the girl?" In this way, signing can provide opportunities to engage your baby in what interests her most.

Comparing Baby Sign Language and ASL

American Sign Language (ASL) is a visual language developed in the United States for use by the Deaf community. ASL has its own unique alphabet, with each letter represented by a specific hand signal. Fingerspelling using these letters can help people who speak ASL identify people and things unique to their own life, such as family and friends' names, pets, or specific places.

Baby sign language is a language that parents develop with preverbal children to communicate.

ASL and baby sign language have many similarities. Both are a series of gestures made with the hands and body to symbolize things, people, places, and ideas. Both are often paired with facial expressions to convey meaning in a more powerful way.

Even though these languages are similar, they differ in a few important ways. Baby sign language is first and foremost a tool to help parents and caregivers communicate with preverbal children so signs can sometimes be approximated or adapted to individual families' needs.

In baby sign language, parents and caregivers improvise hand signals and body gestures in order to communicate with an individual child. For example, if you see your baby slapping the table with his palm to ask for a certain food, you can use a palm pressed to the table instead or paired with the ASL sign.

For parents starting with baby sign language, there are many benefits to using ASL signs rather than completely fabricated signs. The predictable hand shapes and general language rules of ASL will motivate all the signers in a family to use consistent signs. Furthermore, a child who learns ASL gestures will have the advantage of a multilingual communicator as he or she enters school and continues into adult life.

Show Your Feelings

Both ASL and baby sign language rely heavily on facial gestures to convey meaning. For example, the sign for *sad* involves moving flat hands over a very sad-looking pout. The sign would not mean the same thing if the signer were smiling. Since babies react strongly to facial expressions, make sure to show your feelings on your face.

The ABCs of Sign Language

The seeds for modern ASL crossed the sea in the early 1800s from Europe, where the Deaf were making great advances in their ability to communicate through gestures. One of the first steps in creating the language was creating a universal alphabet.

The ASL manual alphabet is meant to be signed using the fingers of a single hand. Each letter has its own unique configuration of fingers and hand shape, and these shapes can be found in many of its signs.

When new concepts or phrases are introduced, or when the sign for a word is unknown, words can be simply fingerspelled. While the manual alphabet might be too advanced for a baby who cannot yet recognize the letters of the alphabet, the hand shapes and finger gestures of the alphabet will allow families to create unique signs when necessary.

Handy Shapes

Common hand shapes taken from the ASL alphabet are interwoven and used in many signed words. For example, to sign *computer* run the "C" hand up your arm. Sign *fruit* by moving the "F" hand against your cheek. Some of the letters in the manual alphabet are more difficult to form, so keep this in mind when working with your baby. Look for approximations of the sign from your baby or toddler.

one hand

Other basic hand shapes include the one hand (just one finger pointing), the open hand (all five fingers out and spread apart), the flat hand (all five fingers out and compact), the curved hand (as though the hand is wrapped around a round object), the bent hand (hand with fingers bent at a 90-degree angle), a clawed hand (with fingers spread and bent), and the *and* hand (with fingers and thumb bent and pinched together).

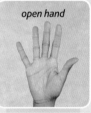

open hand

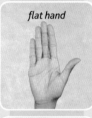

flat hand

bent hand

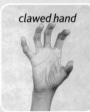

clawed hand

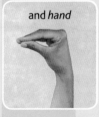

and hand

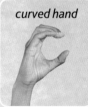

curved hand

Manual Alphabet

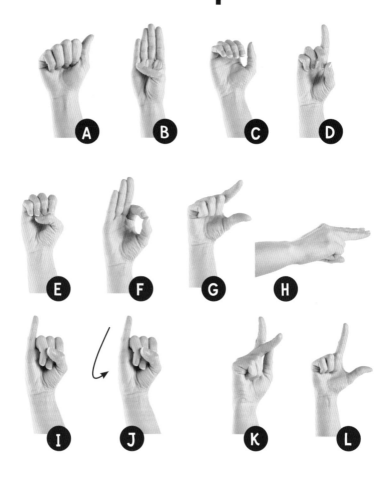

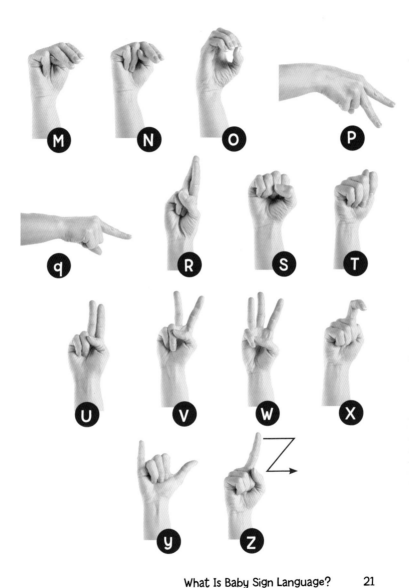

2
Getting Started

It Takes a Village. How many people does your baby interact with each day? In many busy families, babies are cared for by mom, dad, grandparents, siblings, babysitters, and day care providers. It can be challenging to get all of your baby's caregivers to consistently sign with her, but it is worth the extra effort and coordination. If everyone who cares for your child uses the same signs to communicate with her, she will understand and respond to the signs sooner.

Working parents whose children attend day care often find it particularly challenging to get their childcare team on board. If your child goes to a non-signing day care, don't become discouraged. Keep signing to your child, and help coach your day care providers to recognize your child's signs. Some day cares teach their teachers and employees to communicate using signs, so feel free to ask about this practice when considering where to enroll your child.

Tips for Signing in Harmony

To get your childcare team on board, try these tips:

Sign during childcare "handoffs." When your babysitter or a relative arrives at your home, practice signing together. You can hold your baby, wave "hello," and then tell your sitter when your baby last had "milk" (signing *milk*), what he had to "eat" (signing *eat*), or that she'd like to read a "book" (signing *book*). This conversation will reinforce the signs with both your baby and your sitter.

Post common signs around your home. Make copies of the flashcards for common signs provided in this book and hang them around the house in places where a reminder is most useful. For example, post the "diaper" and "sleep" cards in your child's nursery and the "bath" sign near the tub. Everyone who cares for your child in your home will see the signs.

Let your baby be the teacher. When your baby's skill at signing develops, have her teach signs to others, with your help, of course. She will enjoy the opportunity to show off her skills to relatives and friends.

Real-Life Signing

I started signing regularly to my twins Sam and Ben when they were six months old. At around seven months, they returned the sign *milk*, a squeezed, closed fist. At around nine months, they began to sign *eat* regularly, and at ten months, they returned the sign *more*. By the time they turned one year old, they were learning new signs quickly and knew a vocabulary of around ten signs.

The Right Age to Start Signing

Babies begin to communicate as soon as they are born. They cry, move their bodies, and use their hands to get messages across to their caregivers. From birth, babies also begin to associate meaning with the words, noises, and symbols around them. According to most experts, babies between four and six months of age are starting to develop the muscle control and cognitive ability to differentiate signs and repeat gestures.

Starting early with baby sign language definitely has benefits. First and foremost, signing to babies under six months will get parents and caregivers in the habit of signing regularly. The downside is that signing to a baby not yet responsive can be frustrating and make the process seem difficult and unrewarding.

At around nine months of age, most babies have the coordination to start waving bye-bye. Between nine and twelve months, babies master the pincer grasp, which allows them to pick up small objects between their thumb and index finger. Around the same time, babies gain enough control to clap their hands together. These movements are essential to forming many of the early signs. For instance, the sign *more* is made by tapping the fingertips together, and the sign *no* is made by pinching the index finger and middle finger against the thumb.

The "sweet spot" to start signing to a baby is usually between six and twelve months old. Starting with older babies has excellent benefits for parents and baby alike, and as babies get older their coordination and capacity to learn signs increases. Starting earlier has no negative impact other than impatient parents!

Parents don't need to worry about stopping signing at any certain age. As children naturally improve their spoken vocabulary, they will ease out of signing. Continuing to practice ASL even as a child masters spoken language will create a multilingual environment to enrich some families' experiences.

Tips to Get Started with Signing

Choose two or three starter signs that are important to your baby, such as *milk, eat,* or *more*.

Teach your family and other caregivers how and when to make the sign.

Sign to your baby consistently so he can associate the sign with the item or act. For example, try to remember to sign *milk* while nursing or feeding from a bottle.

Be patient. Give your baby lots of time and remember that it could take several months for her to sign back to you.

Praise your child to reward early attempts at signing.

As you're signing, speak the word aloud to give your child both the spoken and signed language.

Use the manual alphabet or combinations of hand shapes to come up with creative signs for names or special objects. For example, refer to Jack by signing the letter "J" and gently shaking it.

Slowly introduce new terms as your baby begins signing back to you.

React to your baby's signs. If she signs *milk*, nurse or offer her a bottle. If he signs *eat*, feed him. This type of cause and effect will help your child understand the power of signing.

Have fun! Enjoy the time you spend with your child and the connection you make while signing.

Using the Baby Sign Language Flashcards

The flashcards that accompany this book are designed as a fun way to learn signs with your baby. Each card features a photograph of me—a real-life mom of three—demonstrating the signs that I have taught to my babies. You'll notice that some signs have two photos and/or small arrows to show the motion of the sign. Remember, baby sign language is not about getting the sign perfect, but rather about finding a way to communicate with your baby.

Studying the flashcards will allow you to learn the vocabulary at home, so that when you see an object elsewhere you'll be able to remember the sign and communicate with your baby. For example, if you see a big truck while out on a walk, you and your baby will both already be familiar with the sign. The cards will give the real-life event even more context.

Use the flashcards as a fun activity with your baby. Go through the deck while snuggling your baby on your lap, or review the cards as an enjoyable addition to story time. You can also get creative and add your own words to the deck. Add signs that you made up for other caregivers by cutting a piece of paper and pasting a photo on one side and a sketch or written instructions of the sign on the reverse side.

dog

Snap fingers of one hand and, with same hand, slap thigh twice, as though calling a dog.

3
Earliest Signs

When your family first begins using baby sign language, it's most effective to choose a few signs that represent simple and frequently-referenced concepts, things, or people. Repeat the signs with your baby until he starts to return the signs. After your baby grasps the first few early signs, begin introducing more, one or two at time. Then move on to more advanced signs. Around six months of age, babies will usually start to recognize the signs, and between nine and twelve months many begin signing back.

Signs representing a baby's early needs are the easiest to learn and to repeat frequently. Many babies begin by signing *milk*, *eat*, *more*, and *juice*. *Diaper*, *sleep*, and *again* are also popular signs to introduce early.

Find a quiet place to sign and make sure your baby can see both your hands and your face. Say the word and make the sign at the same time.

Baby's First Signs

Record your baby's first signs.

Word: _____ First Signed: ___/___/___

Word: _____ First Signed: ___/___/___

Word: _____ First Signed: ___/___/___

Signing During Breast- or Bottle-Feeding

Sometimes it feels like you need three hands to feed your baby, whether you're nursing or bottle-feeding. Getting your child positioned, adjusting clothing, bibs, burp rags, and nipples, can take a lot of coordination. How do you work signing in? Here are a few tips.

Sign *milk* right before feeding time. Making sure your baby can see you clearly, sign and say *milk*, then immediately begin getting ready to nurse or bottle-feed.

Sign and say *milk* once your baby is situated in his nursing position and during a calm moment in the middle of the feeding.

Sign and say *milk* when your baby sees another child drinking a bottle or nursing.

milk

Close and open fist. Think of milking a cow.

eat

Pinch fingers of one hand together. Tap lips.

juice

Make a "J" hand by extending pinky. Touch corner of mouth with pinkie, then flick finger back and away.

more

Tap fingertips of each hand together twice.

all done

Hold open hands at chest level with palms facing you. Quickly flip hands so that palms face out.

yes

Make a fist and bend it twice. Think of a head nodding "yes."

no

Pinch thumb, index, and middle fingers together while shaking head "no."

Signing During Family Mealtime

Family mealtime is an important way to connect with your children and spend quality time together every day. Even before your baby is eating solid foods, you can position the baby swing or seat close to the table so that babies can join the family for their meal. When your baby can sit up in a highchair and eat solids, mealtime can become a fun opportunity to sign together with parents, grandparents, older siblings, and family friends.

Mealtime is also an opportunity to model manners and increase your baby's signing vocabulary, as well as learn and taste new foods. Family mealtime can be a tradition that you continue throughout your child's life, and you can never start too early.

Tips on Early Signing During Mealtime

Say and sign early signs, such as *eat* and *all done*, multiple times as you feed your little one.

Mealtime conversation can be an opportunity to practice signs together. Your baby will be delighted when the whole family signs *more* together, and this is a great opportunity to display the power of signing in action.

As your family gets more advanced with signing, say and sign *please* and *thank you* as you are serving different dishes, handing out silverware, or clearing the table.

please

Place open palm
over heart and make
circular motions.

thank you

Place fingertips on
chin and gesture
outward toward
the person you are
thanking. Smile.

diaper

With both index and middle fingers pointing down and hands positioned at hip level, tap fingers to thumbs to indicate fastening a diaper.

change

Holding both hands in fists, stack wrists together. Then rotate them so the other wrist is on top.

wet

Hold hands up, fingers extended. Then close fingers while pulling hands down.

dry

Extended index finger moves from one corner of mouth to the other, ending with crooked index finger.

hello/ goodbye

In American Sign Language, the signs for *hello* and *goodbye* are made by touching a "B" hand to the forehead and moving it outward, as if saluting. However, most babies say *hello* and *goodbye* using a simple wave that can be with an open hand or by bending and straightening the fingers.

> You can simply point up and down for directional signs.

pick me up

Put both hands up.

hurt

Point index fingers so that they are facing each other and twist them slightly. Position the sign where you feel pain.

bed

Tilt head and rest cheek against pressed palms. Think of sleeping on a pillow.

bath

Rub fists up and down the front of your chest, as though scrubbing yourself clean.

Early Signing During Playtime

Playtime provides many wonderful moments to practice early signs together. These opportunities let you study your baby and learn about his individual interests. Different toys and books give you a variety of ways to demonstrate early concepts.

Tips on Early Signing During Playtime

- Talk to your baby's toys to demonstrate the early signing vocabulary. For example, say and sign, "*HELLO*, Mr. Teddy Bear. Is it time to go to *BED*?" Be imaginative in your play.

- Engage your baby directly with the vocabulary. "Do you *WANT* this rattle?"

- Repeat your baby's favorite games, signing and saying *more* or *again*.

- Sing songs about your baby's favorite toys! Try plugging your baby's name and favorite toy into the tune "Mary had a little lamb."

Careful!

When you sign *toy*, make sure to use both hands. Wiggling one "T" hand is the sign for *potty*. Similarly, wiggling one "Y" hand means *yellow*, but with two hands it means *play*.

play

Make "Y" hands by raising thumbs and pinkies. Twist hands at the wrist a few times. Smile!

toy

Make "T" hands by forming fists and inserting thumbs between index and middle fingers. Shake hands.

ball

Wrap fingers of both hands around an invisible ball.

book

Hold both hands open with palms up and pinkies pressed together. Think of hands as an open book.

music

Holding one arm across body with palm up, use other hand to conduct an invisible orchestra by waving hand back and forth.

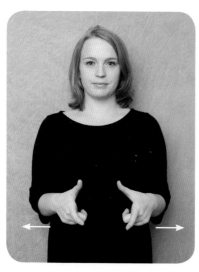

big

Extend thumbs and crook index fingers. With palms facing each other, draw hands apart.

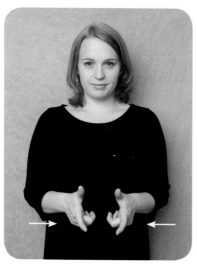

small

Hold hands with palms facing each other. Bring them together toward the center.

Soothing Babies Using Early Signs

When preverbal babies start crying, most parents move through a mental checklist of things that could be wrong. Is it close to feeding time? Could the baby be hungry? Does the baby's diaper need to be changed? Is the baby tired? Overstimulated? The list goes on and on.

As babies mature, baby sign language gives them a way to communicate their needs and gives parents a way to encourage their children to express themselves through signing. The following tips are for babies who have been exposed to baby sign language and/or are around twelve months old.

Tips on Soothing Your Baby with Early Signs

- If your baby starts whining or fussing, make the *what* sign while at eye level. Do this by holding your arms out and bent with your palms facing up. Say, "What's wrong?" They won't be able to respond right away, but after some practice they'll understand what you mean, and be able to express their needs.

- Sign *hungry* and *eat* and watch your baby's reaction. If the baby signs back, or becomes animated and excited, she probably wants to eat. Try offering a snack, signing, and saying *eat* again as you offer the snack.

- Moving through the parents' checklist, sign and say *diaper* and/or *change*, *milk* and/or *thirsty*, or *bed*. When your child reacts to a word or sign, act on it.

- Always praise your baby for any attempts at communicating with you.

- Repeat this ritual whenever your baby begins to whine or fuss. The ritual will give your baby an opportunity to communicate with you and learn how to express her needs.

again

Tap bent fingers onto the open palm of opposite hand.

want

Palms facing up, make claw hands and pull them toward chest while crooking fingers.

help

Place fist, thumb up, on opposite palm. Raise both hands a few inches.

fast

With fingers stretched, place one hand in front of the other. Quickly draw both hands back while making fists.

slow

Slide hand up the back of opposite hand, starting at the fingertips.

stop

Bring edge of hand downward in a chopping motion onto open palm of opposite hand.

Your Baby's First Attempts at Signing

Every single week of the first year of your baby's life, her physical coordination and fine motor skills will improve. So will her capacity to understand the world around her and mimic your actions.

In the early days of signing, you may feel like you're signing and speaking to yourself. Many parents have to remind themselves to be patient and keep trying. Before long, though, you will notice that your baby is recognizing your signs and attempting to sign back.

Here are some things to watch for; they indicate your baby is attempting to communicate through signs:

- Flailing, flapping, and slapping. Your baby may not have the motor skills to mimic the sign yet, but he sees you signing and is trying to repeat the gesture by moving his hands.

- Vocal reactions. If your baby coos, laughs, or squeals when you sign to her, she is responding to your signs.

- Almost there. If your baby puts his hands in his mouth when you sign *eat*, brings a fist to his mouth when you sign *milk*, or claps when you sign *more*, he is trying to sign to you.

Noticing and praising these early efforts will encourage your little one to keep trying until she gets it right. You can help your child by moving her hands into the correct positions and demonstrating the sign again.

How to Praise

Praising your baby's attempts and signs is important to the process. The attention you give him as he begins to recognize and return signs will both reward his efforts and encourage you both to continue mastering early signs.

Verbal praise. "Good job!" "Yay!" "You did it!" Using verbal praise will get your baby excited to keep trying.

Get physical. Pick your baby up; hug and tickle him as a reward for trying to sign.

Use signs. Sign and say *good*, *again*, and *more* to encourage your baby to keep trying.

Their sign is your command. Give babies what they ask for. If she signs *eat*, get her a snack. If he signs *milk*, offer him a bottle or breast. You can give a small snack or just a couple of ounces of milk to cement the cause and effect of the sign without throwing your whole schedule off.

High fives are a great way to show a job well done.

Danielle decided she wanted to teach her six-month-old daughter Maya baby sign language. She'd taught her two-year-old Natalie a few signs and loved the way it empowered her to communicate her needs. She wanted to try even more with Maya.

Real-Life Signing

Life with two little ones was bustling and busy, and Danielle knew that she needed to make a plan if she was going to get started. She talked with her husband Matt and together they chose four signs to start with: *milk*, *more*, *eat*, and *change*.

When Maya was six months, each time Danielle offered her a bottle, she would sign *milk* before and during her feeding. Likewise, when she or Matt fed Maya solids, they would sign *eat*. When Maya had a dirty diaper, she got the *change* sign before being picked up and also while she was on the changing table.

The first three months were a little bit frustrating. Once in a while, Maya would sign *milk*, but Danielle wasn't even sure if it was on purpose or not. Then, between nine and ten months, Maya began signing back. First, Danielle noticed her signing *milk* before she wanted a bottle, then signing *more* and *eat* while sitting in her high chair. After a slow start, the signing became consistent. By the time Maya was around twelve months old, Danielle was able to move on to more advanced vocabulary.

4
Advanced Vocabulary

The vocabulary in this section can be introduced after your baby begins signing the early words. While there is no prescribed time frame for baby sign language, your baby will likely respond best if taught these more advanced signs between twelve and eighteen months. Your family can experiment and test your baby's readiness by weaving a few advanced signs in with early signs to see if your baby's ready to move forward.

Who's Who?

Mommy, Daddy, Grandma, Grandpa, Babysitter, Teacher, Doctor, Aunt, Uncle.... A baby's life is filled with new and interesting people. Some people see your baby on a daily basis, while others only see him once in a while. In ASL, signs that represent females (like *mother*, *aunt*, and *grandma*) are signed below the cheekbones, level with the chin. Signs for males (like *father*, *uncle*, and *grandpa*) are signed above the cheekbones, level with the forehead.

When introducing new people to your baby, make sure your eyes and hands are visible to the baby, make the sign, and say the word. For example, if you're visiting the doctor for the first time, you can keep your baby strapped in the stroller and, standing in front of the stroller with the doctor, say and sign, "Hello, DOCTOR. This is baby Jack." This type of greeting and introduction can help your baby feel comfortable meeting new people.

In this chapter, you'll find signs that identify a few of the most special people in your baby's life. Check the index in the back of the book and the deck of flashcards for more vocabulary and signs about the people in your baby's life.

me

Point to yourself by pressing index finger into center of chest.

baby

Make cradle with arms. Move arms back and forth,
as though rocking a baby.

mommy

With all five fingers extended and spread open, tap chin with thumb.

daddy

With all five fingers extended and spread open, tap forehead with thumb.

brother

Start by signing *boy* by bringing thumb and index finger together in the middle of forehead. Move hand down while extending index finger and thumb to form an "L" hand. Stack hand on top of opposite hand, also an "L" hand.

sister

Start by signing *girl* by running thumb along jaw. Move hand down while extending index finger and thumb to form an "L" hand. Stack hand on top of opposite hand, also an "L" hand.

aunt

Make an "A" hand by creating a fist with the thumb on the outside. Place thumb on jaw and rock slightly.

uncle

Make a "U" hand by holding up index and middle fingers. Move hand in two small circles near temple.

cousin

Make a "C" hand by curving fingers. Shake hand twice next to head.

boy

Bring thumb and index finger together in the middle of forehead, as though touching the brim of a baseball cap.

girl

Run thumb along jaw, as though touching the string of an old-fashioned bonnet.

family

Make "F" hands by rounding thumbs and index fingers together and extending the other fingers. With hands touching at the thumbs and index fingers, swing hands out, around, and back together so that pinkies touch and palms face in.

friend

Hook index finger of one hand over the other index finger. Reverse and hook fingers the opposite way.

Creative Signing

There are many special people in your baby's life who deserve unique recognition. By combining the manual alphabet, hand shapes, and existing signs, you can come up with a sign that's both simple and unique. As your baby gets older, making up signs together can be a fun way to bond with new friends and family members.

For cousin Anders: Sign *cousin* around the forehead to indicate a boy cousin, and then sign the letter *A*.

For Willow, the weekend babysitter: Sign *book* and touch hair with both hands to indicate that Willow reads stories and has long hair.

For playground friend Tommy: Sign the letter "T" and then the sign *friend*.

Remember to say the name aloud as you sign your special names!

Practice Ideas and Learning Games

Make your own custom flashcards! Print photos of the people in your baby's life and sketch or write descriptions of the signs on the back so you can reference them often. You can use the ASL term or a special term you've invented with your baby to identify the person. Shuffle them in amongst the flashcards that accompany this book so you can practice with your baby.

Go through photo albums to show your child the signs for your family members. Point to a person's face and say their relationship and name. For example, "This is Grandma. Her name is Rose." You can then demonstrate the sign for *grandma*, which is made by stepping the *mommy* sign away from the face to indicate multiple generations.

Real-Life Signing

After Annabelle mastered her first signs, her mom, Haley, was ready to start signing about the people in her life. Annabelle's Grandma Kathy lived only twenty minutes away, and babysat often, so Haley made up a sign for Grandma Kathy and taught Annabelle the sign.

Haley created the sign by making the ASL sign for *grandmother*, then adding a peek-a-boo gesture because Grandma Kathy loved to play peek-a-boo with Annabelle.

The other set of grandparents lived in North Carolina, close to the ocean. From her first trip to the beach, Annabelle loved playing in the sand. Once, when Haley was holding Annabelle on her lap and video-chatting with her parents in North Carolina, Annabelle signed *wave*. Her grandparents loved it and henceforth Haley and Annabelle signed *Grandma Wave* and *Grandpa Wave* when they talked about their family members in North Carolina.

grand-mother

Touch chin with thumb of open hand. Then move hand out from chin in two small arches.

grand-father

Touch center of forehead with thumb of open hand. Then move hand out from forehead in two small arches.

Body Parts and Clothing

Around twelve to fifteen months, babies really start to identify their body parts. This type of game is enjoyable for both parents and babies, and adding signs can amplify the fun and the learning.

Teaching babies the signed vocabulary for body parts is helpful, too, as they become more able to communicate their needs. If your baby can express to a caregiver that her head hurts or her tummy aches, the caregiver will be able to treat the ailment faster and with more accuracy. Check the Index in this book and the deck of flashcards for more body signs.

head

With palm down, touch all the fingertips on one hand to cheekbone and then temple.

tummy

With palm up, tap fingertips to stomach.

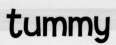

hat

Tap head, mimicking putting on a hat.

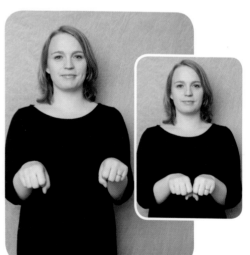

shoes

Make fists with both hands and knock them together twice.

arm

With palm facing down,
slide hand up arm.

leg

Hold closed flat hands
next to leg.

coat

Mime putting on a coat by holding fists around shoulders and bringing them toward the center of chest.

socks

Point extended index fingers down and alternately slide them up and down against each other a few times.

face

Hold one hand with palm toward face, and then move it in a circular gesture around face.

The sign for beautiful is made in almost the same way. To sign beautiful, bring fingertips together to one side after circling the hand around face.

eyes

Point to one eye and then the other.

shirt

Pinch the fabric of shirt
just below the shoulders.

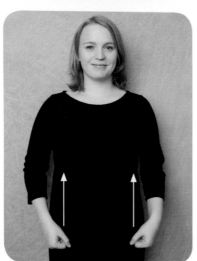

pants

At the hips, pull hands
up toward stomach.
Think of pulling up pants.

Practice Ideas and Learning Games

Sing and sign the popular "Head, Shoulders, Knees, and Toes" song, identifying each of your body parts by both its spoken name and signed name.

Substitute other body parts to create a fun quiz for your baby!

Head, shoulders, knees, and toes, knees and toes.

Head, shoulders, knees, and toes, knees and toes.

And eyes, and ears, and mouth, and nose.

Head, shoulders, knees, and toes, knees and toes.

Real-Life Signing

Jamie's three-year-old daughter Madelyn loves to play with the doctor kit she got for her birthday. She plays with the plastic stethoscope, the toy thermometer, and the Velcro blood pressure cuff. One day, Jamie walked into the playroom and found Madelyn examining her year-old brother Kevin.

Jamie watched as Doctor Madelyn talked a mile a minute to Kevin and asked him to stick out his leg. Kevin ignored her and played with his toy truck. Finally Madelyn walked in front of Kevin and signed *leg* to her baby brother, and lo and behold, he stuck out his leg for an examination. After listening to Kevin's leg with the stethoscope, Doctor Madelyn announced that the baby was in tip-top health.

In the Kitchen

The kitchen is everyone's favorite place to be, at least in most families. There's a special joy that comes with cooking, serving, and eating that brings people of all ages together.

Most babies are highly interested in food and eating—even if they're only willing to eat a few favorite foods—which makes these signs particularly good signs to teach.

Sign while you're preparing and serving, and check in the Index of this book and the deck of flashcards for more food and kitchen signs.

hungry

Make a "C" hand by curving fingers. Slide hand down center of chest.

thirsty

Place index finger on chin and trace a line down throat.

chair

Curve index and middle fingers of one hand and tap them twice onto extended index and middle fingers of opposite hand. Think of sitting in a chair.

cup

Mimic holding a cup by curving your hand.

bowl

Hold both hands palm up with pinkies touching in front of chest. Move hands slightly up and around, as though tracing the outside of a bowl.

spoon

Press index and middle fingers together and use them to scoop out of an invisible bowl held in the other hand.

cold

Hold fists in front of chest and shake them as though you're shivering.

hot

Hold claw hand in front of mouth, palm facing in. Then move hand down and away from mouth.

cereal

Use a curved hand to mime scooping from an imaginary bowl formed from opposite hand.

fruit

Pinching together fingertips of index finger and thumb, create the sign for the letter "F." Bring it to cheek and wiggle it up and down.

vegetable

Make a "V" hand by extending and separating index and middle fingers. Hold index finger to cheek and twist back and forth.

water

Make a "W" hand by extending index, middle, and ring fingers of one hand. Tap chin with index finger.

yogurt

Make a "Y" hand by extending thumb and pinkie. Imagining that the pinkie is a spoon, dip it into an invisible cup held in the other hand and bring it toward mouth.

eggs

Extend the index and middle fingers of both hands. Touch fingertips and then move them down and apart, as though you're cracking an egg.

cookie

Twist fingertips around palm of opposite hand, miming cutting out cookies with a cookie cutter.

cracker

Knock fist against the elbow of opposite arm.

Creative Signing

Is there a food that's a big hit with your child? It's possible that he's already signing to let you know about it. Watch your child for his reactions to favorite foods and see if he has a consistent reaction. Does he slap the table when you take a container of yogurt out of the refrigerator or pat his tummy when he sees you reach for the cheese crackers?

If you see this type of reaction, consider incorporating the movements with the sign you make for that food. You can slap the table and sign for *yogurt* or pat your tummy and sign *cracker*. This can make signing feel fun and let your baby know that you're listening when he communicates with his hands.

Practice Ideas and Learning Games

Take a trip to the grocery store and get your signing hands ready. Put your baby in the seat of the shopping cart and stroll around the store. Start in the produce section and sign *fruit* and *vegetable*. Sign *cracker* and *cookie* in the packaged goods aisle. In the dairy aisle, sign *milk*, *cheese*, and *yogurt*.

Also, look at labels and pictures for other words to say and sign to your baby. Your little one will love the pictures of dogs on dog food cans or the pictures of babies on baby food jars. Looking at these images together will give you another fun opportunity to use baby sign language together.

Real-Life Signing

Dinnertime in Bree's home is the best part of the day, but also the most stressful, and as Bree and her husband Tom hustle to set the table and prepare the meal, their kids often get antsy and frustrated while waiting to eat.

Bree and Tom's three-year old son Dashiell loves to help with the dinner preparations—it makes him feel like a big boy. Lately, Bree has allowed him to mix their fruit salad dessert. While he stirs the mixture, Bree encourages him to sign *apple*, *strawberry*, and *banana* to his one year-old sister, to keep her occupied as well.

"Mom, what's the sign for *hungry*?" Dashiell asks. Bree shows him the sign. "Sisu is hungry," Dashiell explains, speaking for his sister, while making the sign.

When dinner is finally ready, Tom remembers to sign to Dashiell and Sisu.

"Okay, Dash. Now it's time to go wash your hands and sit down to eat."

Tom demonstrates the signs and points to Dashiell's chair.

Animals

Babies love animals. They love the soft fur and sweet nuzzles of dogs and cats and the tight scratchy wool and *baaas* of a barnyard sheep. To a toddler, cold-blooded reptiles and turtles are completely intriguing and the croak and leap of a frog is a fascinating event.

Signing with your baby about animals is a great way to combine his interest in communicating with his passion for the animal kingdom. Be sure to make the sounds of the animals alongside the signs. Check the Index in the back of this book and the deck of flashcards for more animals to sign with your baby.

dog

Snap fingers of one hand and, with same hand, slap thigh twice, as though calling a dog.

butterfly

Cross hands on top of one another. Bend hands at knuckles.
Think of a butterfly flapping its wings.

pig

Holding a flat hand underneath chin, flap fingers up and down.

cat

Hold thumb and index finger together in front of cheek and mime stroking imaginary whiskers.

bug

Extend thumb, index finger, and middle finger of one hand. Hold thumb against nose and flick the index finger and middle finger up and down, like a bug's antennae.

frog

Place fist under chin and flick index and middle fingers twice. Think of a frog jumping.

bird

Place hand against mouth and open and close thumb and index finger. Think of a bird's beak.

duck

Place hand against mouth and open and close fingers and thumb. Think of a duck's bill.

cow

Make "Y" hands by extending thumbs and index fingers. Then hold thumbs against temples to indicate a bull's horns.

fish

Move hands forward in a wavy motion. Think of a fish swimming.

Practice Ideas and Learning Games

The song "Old McDonald" has been teaching children animal noises for generations. Sing and sign the song with your baby to make learning animal signs and noises fun!

Old McDonald had a farm,

E–I–E–I–O.

And on that farm he had an (animal),

E–I–E–I–O.

With an (animal sound) here and an (animal sound) there,

Here an (animal sound), there an (animal sound),

Everywhere an (animal sound).

Old McDonald had a farm,

E–I–E–I–O.

Repeat this verse with different animals and sounds.

Simon and Tamara have a son and a daughter, Felix and Jane. Felix is eighteen months old and loves animals. Jane just turned four and is equally obsessed. Whenever they're out and about and Felix sees a dog, he squeals with delight and barks to get the dog's attention. Jane is gentle and loving when she visits friends with animals.

Simon and Tamara decided one day to visit a big zoo that also had a farm with a petting zoo. They started at the monkey house, where Jane leapt out of the stroller and put her hands in her armpits to sign *monkey*. Felix joined in and made monkey noises.

After they left the monkey house, they visited the petting zoo, the reptile house, and the aviary. But after eating lunch, Felix started getting fussy. Tamara offered him more food and a juice box without success. When he brought his hands to his armpits to

sign *monkey*, Tamara realized he wanted to see the monkeys again. She brought him back to the monkey house while Simon took Jane to pet the sheep one last time.

The Outside World

Honk! Honk! Chugga, chugga, choo, choo! Babies are fascinated by trains, planes, and automobiles. Teaching little ones signs for the different places in the big, wide world—and the ways we get from here to there—can enrich their day-to-day errands and big annual trips.

Look over there! When you and your baby are out and about, encourage them to take it all in.

Whether your baby prefers a walk or a ride in the car, learning the signs will make wherever you go more fun!

look

Point index and middle fingers to both eyes.
Then point fingers in the direction of what
you're looking at.

car

Hold fists slightly in front of you, as though grasping a steering wheel. Then rotate the wheel back and forth.

train

Make "tracks" by pressing the index and middle fingers of one hand together. Make a "train" by pressing the index and middle fingers of the opposite hand together. Run the "train" along the "track."

truck

Fully extending arms, hold fists as though grasping a large steering wheel. Then rotate the wheel back and forth.

airplane

Extend index finger, pinky, and thumb and raise hand above head. Track hand as though watching an airplane fly.

walk

Move hands back and forth to mimic feet walking.

house

Touch fingertips together to form an inverted *V*-shaped roof. Then draw hands apart and down to form the sides of the house.

playground

Make "Y" hands by extending thumbs and pinkies. Twist hands at the wrist a few times. Then with one open hand, palm down, make a couple of counterclockwise circles.

school

Bring palm down onto opposite palm twice.

work

Make fists and tap wrist onto back of opposite wrist twice.

computer

Make the "C" hand shape and place it on the back of your opposite hand. Move the "C" shape up arm.

phone

Hold a "Y" hand to side of face with thumb near ear and pinky near mouth.

rain

Extend fingers of both hands and hold them out and slightly up. Then move hands downward to indicate rain falling.

snow

With fingers spread and palms up, move hands downward while fluttering fingers. Think of snowflakes falling.

sky

Extend flat hand upwards. Look up as you move hand in an arc over head.

umbrella

Mime opening an umbrella by stacking fists and then pulling one fist upward in a smooth motion.

Practice Ideas and Learning Games

Play transportation charades with your baby. Choose a form of transportation and make noises and motions to help your baby guess what vehicle you're acting out.

Try acting out cars, trucks, trains, and airplanes. Sign and say the different transportation vocabulary with your baby.

Real-Life Signing

Justine's baby Gabriel just turned fifteen months old and nothing excites him more than a choo-choo train or a passing bus. Anything with wheels makes Gabriel squeal, laugh, and point. Justine found a DVD that showed all sorts of vehicles, from tractors and subway cars to fire trucks and construction equipment, and it has fast become Gabriel's favorite rainy day activity.

While they watch the video, Justine signs with Gabriel, pausing the video when a new vehicle is introduced. Gabriel mimics the signs and watches, enraptured, as the vehicles roll across the screen. Justine knows that whenever Gabriel signs *train*, he is asking to see the video. When they go out, Justine and Gabriel sign about the different vehicles that they see. A drive around town looking at all the vehicles from his car seat can keep Gabriel occupied for hours—and let Justine get her errands done, which is a big relief.

Feelings and Manners

Expressing feelings and learning manners can be a challenge for babies. Baby sign language creates an opportunity for preverbal children to express their emotions in a way that is easy for caregivers to understand. This type of expression can reduce a baby's frustration and help parents offer more specific remedies.

There are countless opportunities for parents and caregivers to sign about feelings and manners with their children each day. Manners and feelings can be signed during feeding time, playtime, while in transit, and when visiting with family members.

feelings

Bend your middle finger at the knuckle on both hands, and with your palms facing in, move the knuckle around your chest.

like

Spread fingers on chest, then pinch them together as hand moves out and away. Make a happy expression to indicate that you're pleased.

don't like

Start with palm in front of chest and fingers spread. Then pinch fingers together, twist hand, and open fingers again, as though you're plucking something and throwing it away. Make sure your expression conveys dislike.

please

Place open palm over heart and make circular motions.

thank you

Place fingertips on chin and gesture outward toward the person you are thanking. Smile.

I love you

Extend thumb, index finger, and pinky finger straight up. Move hand back and forth.

happy

Place flat palms on chest and sweep hands up using small motions. Make sure facial expression conveys happiness.

sad

With open palms facing you, lower hands from face. Look sad.

surprised

Bring fists to the sides of your forehead and snap index fingers up while opening eyes wide.

grumpy

Using a claw hand, hold hand in front of face. Make a grumpy expression and flex fingers in and out.

shy

Hold fist near jaw. In one smooth gesture, turn head down and to the side, as if hiding.

frightened

Make fists and then quickly open them, fingers outstretched. Open eyes and mouth wide to indicate fear.

tired

Place bent fingertips against chest. Drop hands so knuckles face the floor. Make a tired face.

hug

Cross arms over the chest, as though you are giving yourself a hug.

silly

Make a "Y" hand by extending the thumb and pinky. Hold thumb to nose and wiggle hand back and forth.

funny

Brush nose with index and middle fingers in a downward motion. Smile.

This is a real-life story about me and my kids. When my twins approached sixteen months and my four-year-old got more possessive of his toys, I noticed there was a lot of fighting going on in my home. Before it could escalate to a full-blown battleground, I introduced signs for feelings. I asked that each of the boys sign to the other and that the oldest act as the translator.

Real-Life Signing

The younger boys were happy to feel like their concerns were being heard, and the older boy was pleased to have such an important role in the family's communication. When an argument over a toy arose, the three boys were able to explain their feelings more accurately. Though I still had to intervene and separate them, or take toys away from time to time, everyone was relieved to have a way to communicate complex emotions.

share

Make flat hands. Hold one hand still. Move the other back and forth across the still hand.

5

Continuing Sign Language

Try combining signs to form sentences and more complex ideas. Help your signing baby string signs together to communicate.

Continuing to sign with older toddlers and preschool-age children can be lots of fun. Older children get a lot of satisfaction and enjoyment out of combining signing with the spoken word. You can follow their lead for when to stop, or when to bring more signing into your conversations. However you decide to sign with your child, remember to have fun! Baby sign language can be a rewarding experience for the whole family.

what

With flat hands out and palms up, move hands back and forth and shrug shoulders. Look puzzled.

where

Point extended index finger straight up and shake it back and forth. Look puzzled.

who

Place the tip of thumb on chin with index finger extended. Bend index finger twice. Look puzzled.

why

Touch fingertips of an open hand to forehead, and then bring hand down as you change it to a "Y" hand. Look puzzled.

when

Circle index finger clockwise and down onto opposite index finger. Look puzzled.

how

With your fingers curled, press hands together and twist. Look puzzled.

more

Tap fingertips of each hand together twice.

apple

Bend index finger and twist knuckle against cheek twice.

mommy

With open hand, touch thumb to chin.

play

Shake "Y" hands.

outside

Pinch fingertips together.
Then open hand wide.

brother

Bring thumb and index
finger together in
middle of forehead.
Move hand down while
extending
index finger
and thumb to
form an "L"
hand. Stack
hand on top of
opposite hand,
also an
"L" hand.

walk

Alternately move hands forward and back to mimic feet walking.

dog

Snap fingers and then pat leg.

tummy

Tap fingertips to stomach.

hurt

Touch index fingers together and twist them.

Resources

Books

Holub, Joan. *My First Book of Sign Language*. Scholastic, 2004.

Nelson, Michiyo. *Sign Language: My First 100 Words*. Cartwheel Books, 2008.

Nichols, Catherine. *American Sign Language*. Thunder Bay Press, 2011.

Rosenberg, Karine Shemel. *Baby Sign Language: Find Out What's on Your Baby's Mind*. Sterling, 2006.

Simpson, Teresa R. *Baby Sign Language: Get an Early Start Communicating with Your Baby*. Sterling, 2012.

Journals

Goodwyn, S. W., Acredolo, L. P., & Brown, C. A. (2000). Impact of symbolic gesturing on early language development. *Journal of Nonverbal Behavior*.

Videos

Babcock, Travis (Director). *Baby Signing Time: It's Baby Signing Time*. Two Little Hands Productions, 2007.

Berg, Laura (Director). *Baby Signing in Bilingual/Multilingual Homes*. My Smart Hands, 2012. http://youtu.be/VUKMma5E0uw

Web Sites

Signing Savvy: Your Sign Language Resource **www.signingsavvy.com**

American Sign Language University **www.lifeprint.com**

My Smart Hands: Educating Young Minds **www.mysmarthands.com**

Index of Signs

About the Author

Sarah Christensen Fu is the author of several fiction and non-fiction books for children and adults. She has a master's degree from New York University's program in Media, Culture, and Communication. She is the mother of twin boys and their older brother, and lives in Brooklyn, New York, with her family.